7

Things Young

B
1

Other Books

by
Daniel Whyte III

- *LETTERS TO YOUNG BLACK MEN*

- *LETTERS TO YOUNG BLACK WOMEN*

- *MO' LETTERS TO YOUNG BLACK MEN*

- *LETTERS TO YOUNG BLACK MEN (STUDY GUIDE)*

- *LETTERS TO YOUNG BLACK MEN (LEADERS GUIDE)*

- *WHEN BLACK PREACHERS PREACH, Volume I*, Editor

- *WHEN BLACK PREACHERS PREACH, Volume II*, Editor

- *WHEN BLACK PREACHERS PREACH, Volume III*, Editor

- *MONEY UNDER THE CAR SEAT (AND OTHER THINGS TO THANK GOD FOR)*

- *JUST JESUS! THE GREATEST THINGS EVER SAID ABOUT THE GREATEST MAN WHO EVER LIVED*, Editor

- *7 THINGS YOUNG BLACK MEN DO TO MESS UP THEIR LIVES*

- *GOD HAS SMILED ON ME: A TRIBUTE TO A BLACK FATHER WHO STAYED*

7 Things Young Black Women Do To Mess Up Their Lives

And How to Avoid Them
...with a Word to Parents

Daniel Whyte III
with Meriqua Whyte
And with Special Advice from
Joslyn Neblett, Student Life Department,
Texas Wesleyan University

7 THINGS YOUNG BLACK WOMEN DO TO MESS
UP THEIR LIVES

Cover Designed by Bill Hopper of Hopper Graphics

Copyright 2007
TORCH LEGACY PUBLICATIONS, DALLAS, TEXAS;
ATLANTA, GEORGIA; BROOKLYN, NEW YORK

First Printing, 2007
Second Printing, 2007
Third Printing, 2008

The Bible quotations in this volume are from the King
James Version of the Bible.

The name TORCH LEGACY PUBLICATIONS and its logo
are registered as a trademark in the U.S. patent office.

ISBN Number: 0-9763487-2-1

Printed in the U.S.A.

This book is dedicated to
God,

My daughters:
Daniella, Danita, Danae', Daniqua, Danyelle
and Danielle,

My grand-daughter,
Kywaizia,

And

To all young black women in America and
around the world.

7 *Things Young Black Women Do To Mess Up Their Lives*

CONTENTS

Acknowledgments

First and foremost, I wish to thank my Lord and Saviour, Jesus Christ, for allowing me the privilege to write this book.

I also wish to thank my wife, Meriqua, for helping me to write this book and for editing the book; my daughter, Daniella, for helping with the editing and proofreading process; my son, Daniel IV, for formatting the pages and for helping with the editing and proofreading; my daughters: Danita, Danae` and Daniqua for doing great research on finding the quotes contained in this book; and my two youngest children, Danyel Ezekiel and Danyelle Elizabeth, for being quiet and obedient while I worked on this project.

A very special thank you goes to Bill Hopper and Siouxsie Romack for the wonderful job they did on designing the cover.

Also, special thanks goes to Joslyn Neblett for her wonderful contribution to this book, and for her steadfast encouragement, love, and support.

May the Lord richly bless this book as it goes forth. To

7 Things Young Black Women Do To Mess Up Their Lives

INTRODUCTION

I really believe that many of the problems our young black women face today can be prevented from happening in the first place. Many young black women have seemingly lost their self-respect, so much so that they have subjected themselves to indignities and disrespect, such as allowing themselves to be called out of their name.

The truth of the matter is, many young black women have never been taught and trained in the right way. Many have never been taught how to carry themselves like ladies–with dignity, class and grace. Many have never been taught how to be tough while at the same time remain humble. Many have never been taught how to be strong-minded and not silly-minded, so they fall apart at the slightest misfortune that comes across their path.

Although I strongly believe, according to the Scriptures, that the older women should teach the younger women, I must unfortunately and sadly admit here, that there are not many older women, or older men for that matter, living according to Biblical principles themselves who can, with authority, teach the younger women how to act and how to carry themselves with dignity and class. With that said, I have included in this book what I believe to be seven things many young black women do to mess up their lives.

The purpose of this book is to help young black women avoid messing up their lives by making these seven common mistakes. I believe that any young black woman, who will read this book, and avoid making these seven mistakes, will live a successful and victorious life; one free of unnecessary pain and hurt, and one that will be pleasing to God.

I encourage you, dear sister, to read it and let it become a part of you; then pass it on to another sister so she, too, can get on the right track and stay on the right track with her life, and thus avoid many of the pitfalls that can cause much hurt, pain, and heartache.

—Daniel Whyte III
Dallas, Texas

"Remember now thy Creator in the days of thy youth, while the evil days come not, nor the years draw nigh, when thou shalt say, I have no pleasure in them."

—Ecclesiastes 12:1

"The flower of youth is most beautiful when it bends toward the Son of Righteousness."

Chapter 1

Not Taking God, the Bible, and the Church Seriously

Today, many young black women have forgotten the God of their forefathers and foremothers, and are refusing to take the things of God seriously. By observing the actions of many, one can conclude that they are not thinking of God. Frankly, they are putting God in a box and locking Him out of their lives. Because of this, so many young black women are living depressed and defeated lives.

GOD

One of the reasons why many young black women do not take God, the Bible and the Church seriously is because they have never taken the time to really get to know God for themselves. They know *about* God. They have heard about God, and what He can do, but they have never taken the time to develop a one-on-one personal relationship with Him. They are still relying on the relationship their grandmothers and grandfathers had with God, thinking that somehow it will fall on them by osmosis or something. But it does not work that way.

You are going to have to get to know God for yourself because the day is coming when you, me, and everyone born on this earth, will stand before the Holy and Just God, to give an account for the life we lived while on this earth. You can read it for yourself in Romans 14:11-12: *"For it is written, As I live, saith the Lord, every knee shall bow to me, and every tongue shall confess to God. So then everyone of us shall give account of himself to God."*

You may be wondering: Well, how can I know God for myself? I grew up in the church. My grandmother was on the Motherboard. My grandfather was an usher. My mother is on the Ladies' Auxiliary, so are my auntie and my cousin, and I have been going to church since I have been born, yet you say, I don't know God. Tell me, how can I really know Him personally? I am glad you asked. Here is how to have a personal relationship with Him:

1. The Bible tells us that we are all sinners, and that our sins have separated us from God. We do not make ourselves sinners by doing bad things, rather, we do bad things because we are sinners. Romans 3:23 says: *"For all have sinned and come short of the glory of God."*

2. There is a great punishment for sin and that punishment

is death—both physical death and spiritual death. This spiritual death is actually eternal separation from God in a place called hell. Romans 6:23 tells us: *"For the wages of sin is death..."*

3. Now, you may be thinking, I have done a lot of good deeds, even to people who do not deserve it, don't those good things count? Let's see what Ephesians 2:8 & 9 has to say about our good deeds: *"For by grace are ye saved through faith; and that not of yourselves; it is the gift of God. Not of works, lest any man should boast."* Isaiah 64:6 further tells us: *"But we are all as unclean things and all our righteousnesses are as filthy rags; and we all do fade as a leaf; and our iniquities, like the wind, have taken us away."*

So, you see, dear friend, from these three verses alone, that our good works will not put us in right standing with God.

4. The Good News is, you do not have to pay for your sins. God already made the provision for that when He sent His only Son, Jesus Christ, to come to earth to die for your sins and for my sins. John 3:16 so eloquently tells us: *"For God so loved the world, that he gave his only begotten Son, that whosoever believeth in him should not perish, but have everlasting life."* Jesus Christ came, not to condemn us of our sins, but to deliver us from our sins. John 3:17 says: *"For God sent not his Son into the world to condemn the world; but that the*

world through him might be saved."

5. All you have to do now is simply believe that Jesus Christ died on the cross for your sins, was buried, and rose on the third day by the power of God. John 3:18: *"He that believeth on him* [Jesus Christ] *is not condemned: but he that believeth not is condemned already, because he hath not believed in the name of the only begotten Son of God."*

6. After believing, pray. Ask Jesus to forgive you of your sins, to come and live in your heart, and to help you live for Him. Romans 10:9, 10 & 13 says: *"That if thou shalt confess with thy mouth the Lord Jesus, and shalt believe in thine heart that God hath raised him from the dead, thou shalt be saved. For with the heart man believeth unto righteousness; and with the mouth confession is made unto salvation...For whosoever shall call upon the name of the Lord shall be saved."*

Just pray this simple, but very important prayer if you sincerely believe all that you just read:

Heavenly Father, I come before you as humbly as I know how. I acknowledge the fact that I am a sinner. I believe that Jesus Christ died for my sins, was buried, and rose from the dead. I believe that it is only through Jesus Christ and His shed blood that I can be saved.

Lord Jesus, please forgive me of all my sins, come into my heart and save my soul from sin. Help me to live each day for You from this day forth. In Jesus Christ's name I pray. Amen.

If you prayed the prayer above and made the all important decision to ask Jesus into your heart, congratulations on becoming a part of the wonderful family of God.

Now that you are saved, there are some things you will need to do in order to strengthen your relationship with God, or in other words, to really get to know Him; to really show God that you are serious about Him, His Word and His Church. You will need to:

1. **Pray daily** — Pray in the morning, at noon and at night. Talk to God. Share with Him your heart's desires. Tell Him your joys and your fears. Ask Him to lead and to guide you through the day—each day. Whenever the thought comes to your mind to pray, go ahead and pray; that is the Holy Spirit prompting you to pray, for we have a command to: *"Pray without ceasing"* (I Thessalonians 5:17).

2. **Read the Word of God**. Let God talk to you through His Holy Word. Ask God for understanding and wisdom from His Word. Above all things, ask Him to help you to be obedient to His Word.

3. **Go to Church regularly**. Fellowship with other Christians. The saying goes, Bad company corrupts good behavior. On the flip side, Good company encourages good behavior. So fellowship with other Christians.

THE BIBLE

Another reason many young black women do not take God, the Bible and the Church seriously is because they have become hearers of the Word and not doers. Many, over the years, have become too familiar with the Word of God and thus have begun to take it for granted.

The Bible is a mirror and each time you read it, it shows you your true heart condition. Just as you look into the physical mirror to make sure your hair and clothes are in place, likewise, you ought to look into the mirror of the Word of God to show you your true heart condition. However, many young black women do not want to seriously read God's Word because they know it will convict them and show them what behaviors and actions they ought to change in their life. Hebrews 4:12 tells us: *"For the word of God is quick, and powerful, and sharper than any twoedged sword, piercing even to the dividing asunder of soul and spirit, and of the joints and marrow, and is a discerner of the thoughts and intents of the heart."*

Someone once said, *"Sin will keep you away from the Bible, and the Bible will keep you away from sin."*

Before I became a true, born-again Christian, I could not understand the Bible and so I never took it seriously. I could not understand It because I did not have the Holy Spirit of God to help me. I was depending on my flesh to give me an understanding of spiritual things, and as the Bible says: *"The natural man receiveth not the things of the Spirit of God: for they are foolishness unto him: neither can he know them, because they are spiritually discerned"* (I Corinthians 2:14). Now, because of my own salvation experience, I can say to you the following: see the Bible as God's roadmap to a joyful, fulfilling, and successful life. Read It, study It, and ask God for wisdom in understanding It. But above all else, obey It for therein lies the blessings of God.

THE CHURCH

Another reason why many young black women today, do not take God, the Bible, and the Church seriously is because they became a part of the church, but the church never became a part of them. Oh, yes, you may have been in church every Sunday morning and every Wednesday night, from the time you were a little girl—singing in the choir, helping on the usher board, directing the children's choir, helping Granny clean the church, helping to cook the fellowship dinners, and paying your tithes, but you were doing those deeds out of habit or out of obedience to your parents. You were simply going through the motions. The church never really became a part of you because you really did not see its significance in your life.

Many of our great singers and musicians (out of respect for them I will not name any names here), had their beginnings in the church, but the church never became a part of them, and so after a while they ended up leaving the church and using the talent that God gave them to entertain the world.

I remember as a teenager in High school, I wanted to play on the football team. My mother told me that if I did not sing in the choir, I would not play on the football team at all. I got up there with that choir, and I sang as I had never sung before—just to play football. I was in the church, but the church was not in me. I went to church because my Dad was a leading minister in the church and I was expected to go to church. But because the church was not in me, as soon as I left home, I left the church.

I remember something else that happened in church: One Sunday I was put on the mourners' bench. The leaders and mothers of the church were parading around me, speaking in tongues, trying to get me to speak in tongues. They were not going to let me leave the church until I did that which they wanted me to do, which was to speak in tongues. Well, I got tired of them spitting and foaming at the mouth in my face, and hollering in my ears, "Jesus, Jesus, Jesus." I started shouting and dancing backwards—right out the door.

I did not take the church seriously and because of that, my life took a turn towards that which was not profitable, such as: partying all night, drinking, running women, cursing, and having no regrets nor remorse whatsoever about these things. My life was going in the wrong direction, even though I foolishly thought I was on the right road. And this is what is happening to many young black women and young black men today. I will say here though, that even though I did not care much for God, the Bible or the Church during this time, I would often pray my one sentence prayer: "Lord, show me the light."

God answered my prayer, showed me the light and delivered me from my unprofitable lifestyle. He sent a gentleman to my Air Force dorm room one night, who showed me from the Bible how to get to know God for myself. He showed me the verses I shared with you earlier, and I prayed a similar prayer to the one, that hopefully, you prayed earlier. I can truthfully say, my life took a one hundred and eighty degree turn, and it has never been the same.

So, sisters, let me encourage you to take God, the Bible, and the Church seriously because God does not play, and as the popular saying goes—"God don't like ugly." If you fool around and forget God while you are young, God may just forget you when you get old. Don't play the fool. Play it smart. Make that decision now to live for Jesus Christ and avoid messing up your life.

✓TAKE AWAYS

To avoid this deadly mistake, please take heed to these take aways.

1. Accept Jesus Christ as your personal Saviour.

2. Pray every day, at least three times a day, and then as the Lord leads you.

3. Read, Study, and Meditate on the Bible.

4. Obey what the Bible tells you to do.

5. Attend church regularly. Hang with people who believe in Jesus Christ and who are serving Him.

"If your religion doesn't take you to church, it is doubtful if it will take you to heaven."

"The longer you look at temptation, the more likely you will be to fall for it."

Chapter 2

Following the Crowd and Worldly Vanities

"Vanity of vanities, saith the Preacher, vanity of vanities;
all is vanity."

—Ecclesiastes 1:2

Too many young black women are wearing themselves out, running after the vain pleasures of the world. Many have been misled by the popular saying, "Everybody's doing it." Because of this, many are falling headlong into this worldly pit which they cannot easily climb out of.

One of the main reasons why many young black women are following the vanities of this world, are being led astray, and are thus destroying their lives, is because *they refuse to think for themselves.* I cannot say this enough–THINK FOR YOURSELF! Do not let others think for you. The Bible talks about the broad road that many are on. That road is one of looseness, whoredom, fornication, lies, deceitfulness, rebellion, disobedience, bad attitudes, confusion, hatred, materialism and pain. Out of love and concern for us feeble and sinful human beings, Jesus Christ left these very words of warning with us: *"Enter ye in at the strait gate: for wide is the gate, and broad is the way, that leadeth to destruction, and many there be which go in thereat"* (Matthew 7:13).

Another reason why many young black women are following the vanities of this world is because *there is a void within them that only God can fill, and they are trying to fill that void with other people and the world's material things.* As you read in the previous chapter, it is not until you ask Jesus Christ to save you and you begin living for Him, will you have that void filled. Jesus Christ tells us in John 14:25: *"I am the resurrection and the LIFE: he that believeth in me, though he were dead, yet shall he live."*

A third reason why many young black women are following the vanities of this world is *because of their own sinful, fleshly desires.* Unfortunately, evil is within all of us and we like the temporary pleasure we get from our sins. Little do we know, that sin tends to breed more sin, which breeds more sin, and sin is what messes up our lives. As you may know, the old church folks used to say: "Sin will take you further than you wanted to go, sin will make you pay more than you wanted to pay, sin will make you stay longer than you wanted to stay."

King Solomon, the wisest man who ever lived, had riches

untold. He had everything his heart desired. Solomon tells us in Ecclesiastes 2:1-11:

> *"...therefore, enjoy pleasure..."* (vs 1);
> *"I sought in mine heart to give myself unto wine..."* (vs 3);
> *"I made me great works; I builded me houses; I planted me vineyards"* (vs 4);
> *"I made me gardens and orchards..."* (vs 5);
> *"I got me servants and maidens..."* (vs 7);
> *"I gathered me also silver and gold..."* (vs 8)

But, Solomon goes on to further share with us: *"So I was great, and increased more than all that were before me in Jerusalem: also my wisdom remained with me. And whatsoever mine eyes desired I kept not from them, I withheld not my heart from any joy; for my heart rejoiced in all my labour: and this was my portion of all my labour. Then I looked on all the works that my hands had wrought, and on the labour that I had laboured to do: and, behold, all was vanity and vexation of spirit, and there was no profit under the sun"* (vs 9- 11).

Many of us can identify with Solomon. We are running here and there trying to get this and that, trying to do this and do that, trying to be with the in-crowd, and not pausing to think or to ask ourselves: Is this benefitting me in any way? Is this moving me forward at all?

Solomon had all that his heart desired and yet, he said all his possessions and all his accomplishments were in vain. He was right. I am sure you have heard the old saying, "I have never seen a U-Haul truck following a hearse." Have you?

Below are some of the things that young women get ensnared with:

1. **Trying to fit in with the crowd.** Many young black women try to fit in with the crowd in order to feel accepted. They try to acquire certain material things, wear the latest fashion, use the language and slang common to their peers, and simply try to act "cool." I share with my children all of the time, and I say to you the same thing, "Think for yourself! Think for yourself! Think for yourself!" Follow the Lord and Biblical principles and not what others are saying or doing. Be a leader and not a follower! Remember, "the crowd" crucified Jesus. And the crowd, according to Jesus, is on the broad way to hell. Don't be fooled. This trying to fit in with the crowd often leads to problems with our next point.

2. **Boys.** Some young black women strongly feel that their life is not complete without a boyfriend, and they certainly feel out of the loop and depressed when the girls they hang around have male friends in their lives. It appears that their mentality is, "I just have to have a man, or I'm going to die." Unfortunately, these young women allow themselves to engage in inappropriate behavior with young men, such as petting, kissing, drinking and drugs, which oftentimes leads to losing their virginity at an early age, teen pregnancy, venereal diseases and

date rape, etc. I can go on and on, but I am sure you have heard the horror stories already. This kind of behavior immediately leads to disrespect by the young man, and bad relationships with one's parents. And the strange thing about it all, is the deeper a young woman gets into this pit, the more she will fight to keep the young man who is dragging her down, even to the point of allowing the young man to destroy her relationships with her parents and siblings.

3. **Trying to be something that you're not**. The tattoos, fake hair, and immodest dress only say to others that you are not pleased with how God made you. It also suggests that you are insecure. Sister, be yourself! Enjoy your own company! And listen to your own positive advice, and the advice of your parents, and learn to accept yourself the way God made you, and stop trying to be like somebody else. You are beautiful because you are made in the image of God, and all that God made, He said it is good. Let me encourage you, young black woman, to get on the straight and narrow road. The straight and narrow road is one of honesty, righteousness, humility, pure thoughts, living within your means, abstaining from sex until after marriage, being yourself, hard work, and avoiding bad company.

God has a special job that He wants you to do, but you cannot do that job if you are running with the wrong crowd and following after worldly vanities that lead nowhere. Some years back, the popular singing group TLC sang a hit song called "Waterfalls," and in the chorus, they sang these words:

Don't go chasing waterfalls
Please stick to the rivers and lakes that you're used to
I know that you're gonna have it your way
Or nothing at all
But I think you're moving too fast

So, don't go chasing waterfalls. Don't let the world dictate to you how you should live your life. Think for yourself by following the Lord, because at the end of the day, all that matters is Jesus, just Jesus, and your relationship with Him.

✓TAKE AWAYS

To avoid this deadly mistake, please take heed to these take aways.

1. Follow the Lord Jesus Christ down the straight and narrow road, and avoid the broad way that leads to destruction.

2. Think for yourself! Be a leader instead of a follower.

3. Be yourself. Don't feel like you have to be like other people.

4. Listen to your own advice, and the advice of your parents.

5. Love yourself the way God made you.

6. Do not think your life is incomplete without a boyfriend. And definitely do not allow a young man to touch you until you are married.

7. Stay busy doing things that contribute to your purpose in life.

"Wrong is wrong, even if everyone is doing it. Right is right even though no one does it."

"A child who knows how to pray, work and think is already half-educated."

Chapter 3

Not Taking Education Seriously

Another serious mistake that many young black women make today, is not taking education seriously. Some attend school just to see their friends. Some attend school to play and have fun. Some young women attend school to see the least amount of work that they have to do to get by. And, unfortunately, some quit going to school all together. If you are doing any of the above, you are making a huge mistake.

It is a privilege to get an education and to expand our minds. God has given all of us a beautiful world in which to live, and He wants us to understand His world by learning about it, from a young age. The more we learn about God's world, the more respect and love we have for Him.

The main reason why I believe many young black women do

not take their education seriously is because **they do not see the importance of obtaining a good education**. To them, school is a joke and a place to pass the time. But little do they know that while they are so called passing the time, the time (which they can never get back), has actually passed by and when the day of reckoning comes they are in a daze wondering, what happened?

Some young women still have the mentality that they can skate their way through school and waste time, graduate, and still get a top level position at a law firm. When they don't get that position, they get bitter and upset. There was a time when it was who you know. But not so now-a-days. Your employer wants to know within himself, that you know what you say you know, especially as a young black woman. That degree says to him that you have disciplined yourself and have gone through a rigid course of study and that you know what you say you know. As a young black woman you have to go that extra mile to prove yourself.

Another reason why many young women are not taking their schooling seriously is because, **they do not like to discipline themselves**. Many young women today are lazy and irresponsible. Many do not want to exercise the discipline that it takes to finish well. This leads me to an important point, which is: make your years in school fun. You have to develop within you that internal drive that says, You know what? I have to do this so I might as well make the best of it and have fun doing it. I am going to learn all I can because in the long run I am the one that is going to benefit from it.

The third reason why many young women are not taking their education seriously is because **they have no idea of what they want to do with their life, therefore, seeing no need to learn anything**. I encourage you, at a young age, to decide what you would like to do with your life. Find out what your passion is; that is, what you love to do, and begin setting career goals toward that end.

There are grown people in college as I write this sentence, thirty-five, forty, and even fifty years old who are still working toward getting a college degree because during their young years they did not take their education seriously and after having some sense knocked in their heads they are finally seeing the importance of getting an education. What a waste of one's early life.

The fourth reason why many young women are not too thrilled about getting an education is because **they have the wrong attitude toward education**. All I can tell you here is to change your attitude. Get rid of the negative mentality that you already know everything that there is to know, and that no one can teach you anything. That is a stupid mentality to have. This is one time that you ought to have the attitude of: What is in this for me? What can I get out of this? This is not being selfish because you are in school to learn and the only way that you can learn is by humbling yourself and listening to someone who already knows what you need to know.

I did not take my early years of schooling seriously. I saw school as a place to socialize, to get away from home, and to get into mischief. My friends and I would skip school, turn up late, leave early so that we could do some of the foolish things we wanted to do. I regret that I had such a negative attitude about my early education.

Another reason why many young women are not taking their education seriously is because **they do not like to think and they do not like to work.** They somehow think that knowledge is going to be passed on to them very easily via someone else or some other experience. They have, somewhere along the road, been deceived into thinking that life is a bed of roses. They live a life of dreaming about what they would like to be: an executive in the corner office in some high-rise building on Madison Avenue; the CEO of IBM; or superintendent of the school district. Dream on. But while you're dreaming, put the hard work of thinking and planning and studying behind it; because no dream has ever come to pass without action.

BENEFITS OF A GOOD, SOLID EDUCATION

1. **It will allow you to better express yourself.** You will be able to speak with boldness and confidence, and you will not shy away from, or be too scared to speak to people.

2. **Finishing school will give you a sense of completion,** and a confidence that you cannot gain any other way.

3. **Increasing in knowledge will leave you feeling fulfilled**

even though at the same time you will thirst for more knowledge, and this is good because your education will stem beyond the four walls of the school building.

4. You will definitely be better equipped to help others.

5. Gaining an education will make you feel confident about handling the ups and downs, and the challenges of life and not leave you fearful of the future.

6. A good education will help you do better financially, and materially throughout your life.

7. As you increase in knowledge, you will realize that there is so much more to learn than what you already know. There is a vast world out there and the knowledge that you acquire during your years of school is only the tip of the iceberg.

8. Increasing your knowledge ought to humble you. It is a beautiful thing to see an educated yet humble young woman.

9. Increasing your knowledge will make you a wiser and a more discreet person, and thus will help protect you from the evils of the world. *"When wisdom entereth into thine heart, and knowledge is pleasant unto thy soul; Discretion shall preserve thee, understanding shall keep thee: To deliver thee from the way of the*

evil man, from the man that speaketh froward things" (Proverbs 2:10-12).

10. As an educated young woman, **you will be a discerning woman**; that is, you will be able to differentiate between the good, the bad and the best.

The wisest man who ever lived, King Solomon, said to, *"Take fast hold of instruction; let her not go: keep her; for she is thy life"* (Proverbs 4:13). He further admonishes us to: *"Hear counsel, and receive instruction."* Why? *"...that thou mayest be wise in thy latter end"* (Proverbs 19:20).

✓TAKE AWAYS

To avoid this mistake, please take heed to these take aways.

1. Go to school to learn, not to play.

2. Discipline yourself to study hard.

3. Realize education is a great gift and a great privilege, not a drudgery.

4. Find out what you have a passion for and line up your education to take you in that direction.

5. Take your education seriously, and commit yourself to learning all you can.

6. Have a positive attitude toward education and toward your teachers.

7. Let the benefits of a good education motivate you to do your best.

"If you think education is expensive, try ignorance."

"A modern girl screams
at the sight of a mouse,
but climbs into a car
with a wolf."

Chapter 4

Having Sex, of Any Kind, Before Marriage

"...Now the body is not for fornication, but for the Lord; and the Lord for the body...Know ye not that your bodies are the members of Christ? Shall I then take the members of Christ, and make them the members of an harlot? God forbid...Flee fornication: Every sin that a man doeth is without the body; but he that committeth fornication sinneth against his own body."

—I Corinthians 6:13, 15, 18

Having sex before marriage may be pleasurable, but when the act is over, it yields a lot of heartache and pain down the road. Now, before I go into the reasons why you should not have sex before marriage, let me emphasize here, that a man can only do with you what you allow him to do. In other words, a man cannot have sex with you unless you let him. No matter how much pleading or nice words he uses on you toward that end, no matter how often he tells you he loves you, you are still the one in control. And this is one area of your life that you need to remain in control of.

WHAT IS SEX ANYWAY?

Sex is a pleasurable act that God created for a man and woman who are married to engage in for the multiplying of the human race. There is no mystery to it. A man has a penis, a woman has a vagina, put them together and you have what we call sex. Despite what the world says, you do not have to experiment with sex before marriage to find out how to do it, or to find out whether or not you will like it once you get married. Take my word for it, you will know what to do once you get married, and you will enjoy sex because God made it pleasurable.

Sister, don't get all bent out of shape over this sex thing. Keep your head straight. When you really think about it, the sex act only lasts for a few minutes. Over a lifetime, it takes up about one percent of your life. And I ask you, what is a few minutes of pleasure for a lifetime of hurt? Don't let one percent of your life ruin the other ninety-nine percent. You say, "Oh, he tells me he loves me so many times. He is always buying me stuff." And that is all he is buying you—stuff. I agree with you—he loves you alright. As a man, I know what is in a man so let me tell you what he loves: he loves what he sees; he loves your breasts; he loves the shape of your legs; he loves the roundness of your hips; and he loves the fullness of your lips. But he especially loves what you can do for him in the bedroom.

There is a very thin line between love and lust. True love brings with it respect; a respect that says, even though I may be tempted, I will not fondle her, I will not touch her, I will not kiss her and I will not have sex with her until I marry her. Of course, lust is the complete opposite. True love is a choice and it manifests itself in many, many ways. As the female, you owe it to yourself to demand that respect from the opposite sex. But you have to respect yourself first by saying NO, and always remember, "NO," is a complete sentence all by itself.

SEX IS A SPIRITUAL THING

I believe that sex is a spiritual thing. I cannot fully explain it except for the fact that it was created by God. How does a man and a woman consummate or seal their marriage? By having sex. A bond is created between a man and woman—a bond that cannot be broken no matter how hard one tries to sever it. This is one of the reasons—probably the main reason, why a divorce is so painful and this is why God hates divorce.

I also believe that is the reason why God tells us to flee fornication. In other words, do not have sex with someone you are not married to, because when you go your separate ways, you will try to break that bond that cannot be broken, and that is why you become so hurt, and get so bitter and full of hate when the man "dumps" you after he has used you. You have given him the ultimate that a woman can give a man—her body.

COUNT THE COST

I believe one of the reasons why many young black women are making the mistake of having sex before marriage and thus messing up their lives for years to come, is because they have never sat down and counted the cost. Have you ever asked yourself this question—what will it cost me if I have sex outside of marriage? Let me help you answer that question:

1. **You can get pregnant**. Lest you have forgotten, the only way you can get pregnant is by having sex. Do not fool around and have a child out of wedlock that you are left alone to care for. Oftentimes, the man that you are having sex with will get you pregnant, leave you, and go for another woman because he does not want to get tied down with taking care of you and a baby. Sad to say, a lot of young women today, both black and white, want to lie down and enjoy the pleasures of sex, but do not want to accept the responsibility of taking care of that child that may be born from having sex.

2. **You will bring shame upon yourself and upon your family**. Getting pregnant out of wedlock is still a shameful thing. Your parents and your siblings also undergo some amount of embarrassment. Don't hurt your good name and don't bring shame upon your family.

3. **You will be seen as a whore.** Don't get mad at me. That is what the Bible calls women who have sex with people they are not married to. Your so-called friends will refer to you in that way behind your back whenever they talk about you. The boy who had sex with you will go back to his buddies talking about you like a dog: "Oh, she ain't about nothing. She is as loose as can be. I got her." Then other boys start thinking they can get you too, and will get mad if you do not cooperate.

4. **You will be seen as easy and worthless.** The man or boy who is having sex with more than one woman, or who has had sex with more than one woman and who has one or several children out of wedlock, is somehow, in our society's twisted way of thinking, placed on a pedestal, and seen as a "real man." But not so for a woman who has had sex outside of marriage— even if it is just a one time affair. Her value goes way down in the sight of some people. I know this is not fair, but unfortunately, that is just the way it is.

5. **If you have any hopes of getting married you had better contain yourself.** You don't see the wives of these hip-hop artists out there shaking their hips like the girls on the hip-hop videos, do you? No, in many cases, their wives are the nice hometown girl who kept herself for marriage, and who is home, taking care of the children. These same rappers do not want their precious wives and daughters out their shaking their behinds, but they don't mind you doing it for them. That is strange, isn't it?

A man, even the worst of them, when it comes to having a

family and settling down, wants a virgin. He does not want a woman who has been pawed all over by other men—even if it is just one man. Oh, yes, he may have messed up other women's lives, but strangely, he doesn't want his wife to be a woman that has been had by other men.

6. **You will carry pain and hurt with you for a long time.** You will always remember the man or men you had sex with, and how you got hurt by what you did together. This kind of pain, hurt and shame can stay with you for a long time.

7. **Understand that there are some "dawgs" out there.** They are ruthless and their main aim is to use you to get what they want. They have no respect at all for the opposite sex. Their only concern is their own pleasure and fulfillment. They are heartless. Don't think because he listened patiently to your problems and home situation, that he cares about you. He only sees you as easy prey. Men love to prey on a woman's emotions, taking advantage of her to satisfy themselves. (Please see my chapter entitled "Beware of the Dawgs" in my bestselling book, *Letters to Young Black Women*.)

8. **Venereal Diseases are still out there.** AIDS is still at the top of the list, but there are many other venereal diseases out there as well. You don't want to fool around with a man, not knowing who else he has been with, and end up with a lifelong disease.

9. **If you do get married, the question is going to come up— Have you ever had sex with another man?** A man who is about anything will ask you this question before he marries you or

early on in the marriage. You can't lie because as soon as he has sex with you, the truth will be revealed to him. How? The first time a woman has sex, the hymen, or the covering over the opening leading from the vagina into the uterus (where the baby develops), gets broken and you shed blood. That will be proof to him as to whether or not he is the first person you have had sex with. So if the question ever comes up, just tell the truth.

HANDLING SEXUAL TEMPTATIONS SO THAT YOUR LIFE WON'T GET MESSED UP

You may be saying, the temptation is out there, and it is hard to handle. That may be true, but let me add here that I am not trying to take away your fun. I am only saying to you that, you will have more fun if you wait until you get married to have sex.

Here's how you handle the temptation to have sex before marriage and not mess up your life:

A. Make up your mind, from jump street, that you are not going to have sex before marriage under any circumstances. Pray about it daily and ask God to give you the grace to remain chaste until you get married. He will do His part because what you are asking of Him is pleasing to Him and will bring glory and honour to His Name.

B. Never go anywhere alone with a man. Don't put yourself

in a position where something bad can happen. The Bible says in Ephesians 4:27: *"Neither give place to the devil."*

C. Always let your parents know where you are and who you are with. Make yourself accountable to them.

D. Have the mindset that, getting pregnant before marriage is a shameful thing. That being the case, stay away from sex before marriage.

E. Dress modestly. That is, wear clothing that covers you up. Let your clothing be one of virtuousness and obedience to the Word of God. By the way, a woman actually looks more attractive to a man when she is dressed modestly. You may not believe that, but it is true.

F. Never let a man touch you or kiss you in any way, shape, form or fashion. Women respond to touch, and if you are not strong enough to say, "no," you will fall into their trap.

G. Stay busy. I cannot emphasize that enough. Keep your mind occupied at all times with good, wholesome things. Paul encourages us in Philippians 4:8: *"Finally, brethren, whatsoever things are true, whatsoever things are honest, whatsoever things are pure, whatsoever things are lovely, whatsoever things are of good report; if there be any virtue, and if there be any praise, think on these things."*

H. Set lifelong goals. Stay focused on your goals. Do not

look to the left or to the right. I believe the devil sends men into some women's lives to divert them from their worthy goals, and to ruin their testimony for Jesus Christ. *"Let thine eyes look right on, and let thine eyelids look straight before thee. Ponder the path of thy feet, and let all thy ways be established. Turn not to the right hand nor to the left: remove thy foot from evil"* (Proverbs 4:25-27).

I. Get out of your mind, that you have to have a man in order to have a good life. The truth is you really don't need anybody but the Lord. What I would encourage you to do is set your career goals, get your Masters degree and work towards your Doctorate, and take care of yourself and help your brothers and sisters along the way.

J. If you have any desire for marriage, pray daily and ask God to send you a good man. Don't go looking for a man or you will get burned. Men get turned off by desperate women.

And just in case you have already messed up your life by giving up your virginity before marriage, all I can say is, don't beat up on yourself because if you have confessed your sin God has forgiven you, but He does not want you to continue in that sin. Pray yourself through this tough time, pick yourself up, accept it, and move on with your life, and don't let it happen again. If the devil or other people throw it in your face, just say, "Yes, it happened, but God has forgiven me and if you cannot deal with that maybe it is not meant for us to be together."

✓TAKE AWAYS

To avoid this deadly mistake, please take heed to these take aways.

1. Avoid having sex, of any kind, before marriage.

2. Do not let a man touch you, kiss you, or fondle you in any way, shape, form, or fashion until you are married.

3. Do not look for a man. If you desire to get married, pray to God and ask Him for a mate.

4. Keep your mind occupied. Stay busy with your goals.

5. Never hold a conversation with any man beyond what is necessary. And never hold a private conversation with any man.

6. Make yourself accountable to your parents or someone you respect. Let them know where you are and who you are with at all times.

7. Make up your mind, before time, what you are going to do when the temptation comes.

"The girl who has
many men on a string
will soon get into
a tangle."

"Family happiness is homemade."

Chapter 5

Not Appreciating Your Parents or Family

I believe, in this day and time, especially in light of the fact that things are getting worse around us, that families ought to stay together, pull together, and encourage each other, no matter what the situation. But I see in some young black women a lack of appreciation for their family. Some are unwilling to place themselves under the rule and leadership of their parents. Parents do have the authority, from God, to question you about anything they wish. Accountability will help keep you on track and will, in a way, force you to live right. However, many young black women do not want to be accountable to anyone including their parents. Below are some of the reasons why:

1. **Many young black women think they know it all.** They are so proud, they cannot see how ignorant they really are. Proverbs 12:15 says to people who think they know it all: *"The way of a fool is right in his own eyes: but he that hearkeneth unto*

counsel is wise. "Because you think you know it all, you refuse to listen to the instruction of your parents. The Word of God says: *"A wise son* (or **daughter**) *heareth his* (or her) *father's instruction: but a scorner heareth not rebuke"* (Proverbs 13:1). Your parents have been where you are trying to go. They may have made some mistakes along the way, and they are only trying to prevent you from making the same mistakes.

I am not pointing the finger, because when I was your age, I used to be full of pride, thinking I knew everything. But I soon found out through the hard punches of life that having this kind of attitude was not the way to go, especially if I wanted to find favour in the eyes of God and man.

2. **Some young women want to continue in the sin that they are involved in.** Some know that their parents will not approve of the friends they have. They know their parents will not approve of the places they hang out, and so they resent it when their parents question their whereabouts, etc. And they try to use their bad attitude to control their parents into letting them have their way. But remember that the Bible says: *"Be sure your sins will find you out"* and also, *"You reap what you sow."* If I were you, I would subject myself to my parents and avoid a lot of trouble.

3. **Familiarity breeds contempt.** The fact is, some young black women have become too familiar with their parents—they know their faults and failures, they see their shortcomings and their inconsistencies—that they, somehow feel they do not have to listen to their parents or older siblings. There is going to come

a day, however, when your parents are going to stand before God and give an account to Him as to the kind of daughter you have been while living with them. If you don't believe me read Hebrews 13:17 for yourself: *"Obey them that have the rule over you, and submit yourselves: for they watch over your souls, as they that must give account, that they may do it with joy, and not with grief: for that is unprofitable for you."* Wouldn't you like for your parents to give a good report of you? Young ladies, you have a promise from God in Ephesians 6:1-3 that if you respect and obey your parents, you will live a long and blessed life: *"Children, obey your parents in the Lord: for this is right. Honour thy father and mother; which is the first commandment with promise; That it may be well with thee, and thou mayest live long on the earth."*

"Children, obey your parents in all things: for this is well pleasing unto the Lord."
—Colossians 3:18

"Honour thy father and thy mother: that thy days may be long upon the land which the Lord thy God giveth thee."
—Exodus 20:12

I don't know about you, but I want to live a long and blessed life. Sisters, if you want to live a long and blessed life also, may I encourage you to realize the blessings of being submissive to and responsible to your parents. Do your part by being obedient and God has riches in store for you.

You may be thinking, you don't know my family situation. You are right. I do not know your family situation, but this one thing I do know, and that is, no matter what your home situation, there is always someone in a worse situation than you are in.

Let me encourage you to take the initiative, and do your part to create a stronger bond with your family. Below are a few ways in which you can create that bond. Pray over each of them and with God's help implement as many as you can:

1. Share with your family your dreams and desires.

2. Share with them, in a humble way, some things that may be frustrating you, your likes and dislikes, and even your fears.

3. Ask your parents questions. Find out what it was like growing up for them.

4. Spend some time in the kitchen with your mother. Cook, bake, and clean up with her.

5. Play with your younger brothers or sisters, if you have them. Answer their questions. Don't get frustrated with them because you are their first role model. Enjoy them and realize that you can have a great positive impact on their lives.

6. Share the contents of a book you are reading with your parents. Discuss some historical events with them.

7. If you are interested in a boy, share that with your parents. Don't be secretive about it. They can and will be delighted to lead you in the right path regarding that vital subject.

8. Go to church with your family.

9. One of the ideal settings to converse with your family is at the dinner table. Hopefully, you all eat at least one meal together. If this is not the case, bring that up with your family as a matter of concern.

10. Bring your friends home instead of you always going over to their house. They may never say it, but some people get tired of non-family always hanging out at their place. Remember this verse: *"Withdraw thy foot from thy neighbour's house; lest he be weary of thee, and so hate thee"* (Proverbs 25:17).

Young woman, build memories with your family by filling in the gap. Appreciate your family and do not take them for granted because they can be here today and gone tomorrow.

✓TAKE AWAYS

To avoid this deadly mistake, please take heed to these take aways.

1. Listen to the advice of your parents.

2. Respect, honor and obey your parents.

3. Love your siblings.

4. Communicate with your family.

5. Be accountable to your parents.

6. Take the initiative to draw closer to your family.

"Don't treat your family like a pit stop on the raceway of life."

"Though it rains gold and silver in a foreign land and daggers and spears at home, yet it is better to be at home."

Chapter 6

Leaving Home Too Soon

God provides the home and sets the family up to be a safe haven from the hustle and bustle of the world. Home is where you are groomed and trained to face life once you are grown. Home is the safest place to be until you reach the age of maturity where you can then face the world with confidence. Sisters, I encourage you not to be in a hurry to leave the comforts of your home—no matter how bad you think the situation may be.

I strongly believe that as a young black woman, you ought to stay home until you get married. I know this sounds old fashioned, but it is the wisest thing that you can do. God has provided two protections for you as a woman—that of your parents and the other of your husband.

There are men out there who are watching women, waiting to pounce on them. You say, "Oh, I can handle these men. I can take care of myself. I can go it alone." Many young ladies have left home thinking they can handle these men, and the other problems of life that beset young women, but they found out the hard way that they couldn't. They have come back home crying to Mama. Some are out there still crying, too proud to admit they have messed up. So my advice to you, dear sister, is, stay home until you get married.

Despite what the world might tell you, eighteen years of age is not full maturity. At eighteen, you are just beginning to knock on the door of full maturity.

TRUE MATURITY

What is true maturity anyway? Maturity, according to developmental psychologists is when a person responds to his/ her circumstances or environment in an appropriate manner.

MARKS OF A MATURE WOMAN

One mark of a mature young black woman is **she has a positive attitude**, no matter what. A mature woman does not fall apart when things go wrong. She learns to look on the bright side of things. She takes a bad situation, turns it over in her mind, learns from it, looks for any good in it, and keeps on going.

If you are one of those young women who fall apart when

things do not go your way, then you need to stay home with your parents until you get that part of your life under control because things are not always going to go your way in life.

A second mark of a mature young woman is, **she will try not to make the same mistake twice.** If you have messed around with a fellow you are not married to and got pregnant, then maturity will say, "I am not going to do that again." (Get a copy of T.D. Jakes' message, entitled, "I Bet You I Won't Do that Again.")

A third mark of a mature young black woman is, **she is a listening person.** She knows when to listen and when to speak. As one wise older lady once told me, "You tell a little but you keep a little."

Another mark of a mature young woman is **she is a disciplined person.** She has self-control, character, and orderliness in her life. She also knows how to stay focused on the task at hand.

The fifth mark of a mature young black woman is, **she is a responsible person.** I remember when I was about seventeen years old, and I had borrowed my mother's new car. She trusted me with it. Anyway, my buddies and I, in the process of carousing around town, put a big dent on the side of her car. Rather than doing the responsible and mature thing, and telling her about it, I parked the car in the driveway as though nothing had happened. She did not notice the dent the next day when she drove the car to work. I got my buddies together around 10:00 that morning, we went to her job, and there in the parking lot, we tried to fix the dent with a rubber hammer.

Little did I know, my mother was on break then, and she just happened to look out the one window that the building had, and she was shocked to see her oldest son and his gang beating on her new Grenada (and back then, the Grenada was the black man's Mercedes), rather than coming to her and telling her about the problem. She was very disappointed. That, my friend, is not an act of maturity, but one of immaturity and irresponsibility.

A sixth mark of a mature young black woman is, **she acts on facts and not on her emotions**. Maturity will say, "Yes, I may feel this way but the fact is..."

Young ladies, stay home and don't be in a hurry to leave home. The devil will blind your eyes by showing you the flashing lights and the fast-paced life of others. Always remember, "don't go chasing waterfalls."

✓TAKE AWAYS

To avoid this deadly mistake, please take heed to these take aways.

1. Thank God daily that you have a place to call home.

2. Always have a positive attitude, no matter what your home situation is, because things could be worse.

3. Stay at home until you are married.

4. Be mature in your attitude, your actions, and your words.

"The future belongs to those who prepare for it."

"Unless you assume a God, the question of life's purpose is meaningless."

Chapter 7

Not Having Clear Direction in Life

There is a saying that goes like this: "People who fail to plan, plan to fail." That is so true. If you fail to set daily, weekly and lifelong goals, you are setting yourself up for failure. You cannot just hop out of bed each morning, running here and there, not knowing which way to go and expect to get much, if anything, accomplished. At the end of the day you will look back and wonder, where has the time gone? What positive thing have I accomplished? You will feel that you just wasted that day, and if you do that every day, you will eventually waste your whole life.

I strongly believe, as a young person, you should have some idea of what the Lord wants you to do with your life. In order to keep yourself out of a lot of confusion and lost time, you need to find out what you are gifted at and what you really enjoy doing, and pursue it with all of your might.

Setting solid goals will keep you on track. Setting goals will give you a reason to live each day. They will add excitement to your life as you work toward accomplishing them, striving to overcome obstacles that may be in the way. There is a great feeling of self-fulfillment and accomplishment when you reach a goal. Even the Bible tells us in Proverbs 13:19a that: *"The desire* [or goal] *accomplished is sweet to the soul..."*

Verse twelve of that same chapter says: *"Hope deferred maketh the heart sick: but when the desire cometh* [or the goal is reached] *it is a tree of life."*

Obstacles in reaching your goals are to be expected and that is a part of what makes accomplishing a goal exciting. These obstacles may be external or they may be internal.

EXTERNAL OBSTACLES

An external obstacle may be, a friend wanting you to spend your hard earned money, that you were putting away to complete college, to get an apartment. You have to risk that friendship by telling that friend "no" in order to reach your goal that you made for your life, which was to go to college.

Another external obstacle may be the partying that takes place each weekend. You are going to be strongly tempted to go because it requires no effort on your part when compared with the studying you have to do that weekend. This also, however, is an obstacle to which you have to say, "No!"

Another external obstacle which many young black women, sad to say, are stumbling over is a boyfriend. Yes, my dear sisters, your boyfriend can be an obstacle. Don't let him be. You have set a goal to get your degree before you get married, but your boyfriend wants to get married now. You have to firmly say to him: "I have a goal to reach and you are not going to stand in my way. Either you travel alongside and help me reach it so we can have a better life together, or say with Ray Charles, 'Hit the road, Jack.'"

Yes, you are going to meet some external obstacles along the way. It's not going to be easy. But then, nothing worth having in life comes easy or free.

INTERNAL OBSTACLES

Then there are internal obstacles. These, in my opinion, are the hardest to overcome because they come from inside you and can become so much a part of you.

The first of these internal obstacles is **procrastination**. Procrastination is putting off that which you know you ought to do right now. "I'll do it tomorrow," you keep telling yourself. The problem is, tomorrow will always be tomorrow and never today. Later will always be later and never now. A part of excellence is not procrastinating. When you procrastinate you steal time from yourself because then you end up rushing to get a particular job done or you end up not doing it at all because of the stress involved in rushing to get it done. So do not procrastinate.

One good way to avoid procrastination is to write things down. Live by lists. Write down what you have to get done that day or that week and you will have such a good feeling crossing things off as you get them done. At the end of the day when you look over that list you will not feel like you wasted that day.

A second internal obstacle to overcome is **laziness**. Procrastination and laziness go hand in hand. Laziness says, "I don't want to." Laziness says, "Not now." Laziness sees all the negatives of life. Laziness sees all the obstacles in the way and does not put forth an effort to find a way to get around the obstacle. Proverbs 22:13 tells us: *"The slothful man sayeth, There is a lion without, I shall be slain in the streets."*

I live a writer's life. To write this important book I have had to overcome procrastination, lose sleep, skip meals, eat off schedule, spend long hours in solitude and focus in on the job at hand. A lazy mentality would not have lent itself to helping me accomplish the task of finishing this book. Same goes for you.

Have you ever heard the story of the little engine? The little engine stood at the bottom of the steep hill, looked up to the top and started with an "I think I can, I think I can" mentality. Huffing and puffing, it started up the hill. Half way up the hill the engine said, "I know I can, I know I can." It kept saying those words until it reached the top of the hill. Once at the top, it tooted its horn and yelled, "I did it!" Have the same mentality as that little engine because you can do anything you set your mind to.

Below is a poem my daughter copied and taped on the wall above one of our computers. It reads:

> "I can't" is a quitter
> "I don't know" is too lazy
> "I wish I could" is a wisher
> "I might" is waking up
> "I will try" is on his feet
> "I can" is on his way
> "I will" is at work
> "I did" is now boss

A third obstacle to goal setting is **fear**—fear of failure, fear that you will not reach that goal, fear of the unknown. But if you pray and seek God's wisdom and guidance as you plan, then you have nothing to fear. Remember what the Apostle Paul said in Philippians 4:13: *"I can do all things through Christ which strengtheneth me."* You have a promise from God, Who does not lie, that if you, "Trust in the Lord with all thine heart; and lean not unto thine own understanding. In all thy ways acknowledge him, and he shall direct thy paths."

A fourth obstacle may be **illness**. Don't let that stop you completely in your tracks. You may have to slow down or temporarily stop, but after the illness passes, "gird up the loins of your mind" and start running again towards those goals.

PRIORITIZE YOUR GOALS

Before setting your goals, always remember to first pray, then think, then do. Prioritize your goals:

1. Do the most important things first.
2. Do the most unpleasant task next.
3. Do the largest and most time-consuming task before you do smaller, less important, and less time-consuming tasks.
4. Be flexible. Realize that things are going to come up that will throw you off schedule. Learn how to adjust your schedule. Learn how to reset your goals. Learn how to stop, deal with an obstacle and then move on.
5. Reward yourself after reaching a goal.

Young ladies, don't mess up your life by living a dry existence with no clear direction. If you don't have something to live for, you will fall for anything that crosses your path, and not everything that the world has to offer is good for you. Don't let others live your life for you, pulling you here and there. You take charge of your own life and set your own agenda because you are the one who has to live with the results.

✓TAKE AWAYS

To avoid this mistake, please take heed to these take aways.

1. Pray! Think! Do!

2. Set goals and pursue them with all your might.

3. Live by lists. Write down what you have to do and refer to your list throughout the day.

4. Do not fear anything or anybody.

5. Have a "do things now" mentality.

6. Do not be lazy. Get up early and work hard to get your goals accomplished.

7. Prioritize your goals.

8. Overcome external and internal obstacles that may be in your path.

Special Comments from a Fellow Young Black Sister

by Joslyn L. Neblett

NOTE: Dear Reader, I have asked a dear young lady by the name of Joslyn Neblett, who is actually successfully living out the Biblical principles that I expound on in this book, to add her comments to this book, so as to encourage you, from the perspective of a young black women, who is actually doing it, to apply these success principles to your own life so that you can live a life of power, joy, victory, and without regrets.

—Daniel Whyte III

Special Comments for Young Black Women

by Joslyn Neblett

Dear Sisters:

I hope that all is well with you on this blessed day. As for me, everything is just wonderful.

According to Daniel and Meriqua Whyte, *"Too many of America's young black women are making the wrong decisions and are going down the wrong paths."* Outlined in this book are common mistakes young black women have made and are making that is causing them to mess up their lives.

This is a repertoire for women, in hopes of diminishing unfavorable mistakes. The purpose of this book is to direct women down the path of righteousness, and in doing so a productive and successful life is spawned.

As a young black woman myself, may I admonish you to take heed to the many things mentioned in this book. It is time for you to take a stand. You have been overshadowed for too long. You have more to offer the world than you think. Tap into your God-given abilities. Start respecting yourself and be self-confident, knowing that God is too wise to make a mistake. You were made in His image and this alone demonstrates you are special. You're not an accident. God created you on purpose. Step into your destiny and remember, *"...the violent take it by force."*

I hope that you find this book informative even as I did. This remarkable project was laid on the hearts of two of God's finest in the ministry–a great man and woman, Daniel and Meriqua Whyte. From the bottom of my heart, I would like to thank the both of you and your children for welcoming me into such a blissful family and also for providing me with the opportunity to speak for the Lord. My desire is to impart knowledge into the minds of God's people, as I too, continue to learn and grow.

With Love,

Joslyn L. Neblett

CHAPTER 1
On Not Taking God, the Bible, and the Church Seriously

What <u>causes</u> us to put God in a box and lock Him out of our lives? To reiterate what Rev. Whyte expounded on earlier on this subject, some feel as though they can make it without serving the God of Ages Past, the Sustainer of our forefathers and foremothers. Because the elder generation has paved the way, today's contemporaries think there is not a need to seek and labor for God in the manner in which they did long ago.

On the other hand, there are those who also feel that there is not a need to live holy and committed lives. For instance, I have overheard people make comments justifying unrighteous living. One comment in particular is: "It doesn't take all of that." The truth is, my friend, it takes all of that and more, preferably a *willing spirit*, according to what Jesus Christ said in Matthew 16:24, ***"Then said Jesus unto his disciples, If any man will come after me, let him deny himself, and take up his cross, and follow me."***

NO ONE WANTS TO BE HELD ACCOUNTABLE

Another reason why I strongly believe people want to lock God up in a box is because most people do not hold themselves accountable nor do they want to be held accountable for their decisions and actions. To many people, it is acceptable to live like the devil Monday through Saturday, and act like a saint on Sunday–at least until one leaves the House of God.

The Bible

Though the Bible is deemed as an essential source of information inspired by God Himself, there are those of us who fail in the area of exposing ourselves to the words of life contained therein. Listed below are the most commonly used excuses that young women give for not exploring the Bible:

1. **Too many words on the page**. Many of us do not read the Bible because we feel that there are too many words on the page, yet we choose to read a magazine, in most cases filled with pornography and explicit graphics.

2. **I just don't understand It**. There are those of us who cannot make sense of the Bible, or understand the words of wisdom being spoken. Perhaps one could consult their pastor, a fellow church member, or even another rendition of the Bible to help them understand the message at hand.

3. **I am just too tired**. There are also those of us who become heavy-eyed each time the Good Book is opened. If the truth be told we are fooling ourselves, because there are plenty of

things that we gaily do in place of not reading the Word.

4. **I don't have enough time**. Sometimes we find that there are other things we have a desire to do. For example: If you are a student, parent, or employee, etc, there will always be the ins and outs of a customary lifestyle, and because of this, we choose not to make time to read the Bible.

Even if these are justifiable excuses, this still does not exempt us from spending time with God. Such confessions demonstrate that we are a society with many excuses. We pick and choose the things that are priorities in our lives. No matter the reason you give for not breaking open the *Bread of Life*, just know that it is time to start anew. Pray and ask the Lord to give you insight regarding His Word, meditate upon it, and then apply it to your life daily.

The Word at Its Best

The Word of God itself is conscientious. In order to provide a better understanding of the Bible at work, I have simplified things by creating an illustration. This includes different professions (P) and their daily routines with an analogy (A) to the Bible:

P. Doctor: Treats patients stricken with ill-health.
A. Bible: It is the prescription that never expires; it medicates any ailment that arises in your life.

P. Chef: Adds several ingredients into a recipe to bring out its tastefulness.
A. Bible: It is the flavor of life; no extra ingredients needed.

P. Firefighter: Extinguishes fires caused from grease, chemicals, etc.
A. Bible: It puts out life's sweltering fires, regardless of intensity.

P. Mountaineer: Compasses life's path.
A. Bible: It is the compass that leads to life's path, no matter the surface.

The Bible is the best remedy to any sticky situation in your life. We are challenged by God to become more than just *hearers;* we must also be *readers of the Word*, and more importantly, *doers of the Word*.

Why the Church Isn't Taken Seriously

In my opinion, the most poignant reason for young black women, or people in general, not taking the church seriously is *because of the hypocrisy in today's times*. Although there were disquieted issues that existed long ago within the sphere of the church, the same double standards are rapidly arising today. For example, various church scandals involving many of our well-respected pastors have become a problem. However, you must not keep your eyes on men alone. The Pastors, Bishops, Apostles and Prophets are merely individuals being used by

God. Being that they are only human the idea of them making mistakes, or falling into pits, is not far-fetched.

Another reason the church is not taken seriously is due to the same idea Rev. Whyte expressed previously, and that is: *People attend church but don't allow it to become ingrained into them.* Aside from tradition, the average church-goer goes to church out of habit and not out of love for God. Most of us feel that if we give God some of our time He'll be satisfied, but that is not the case.

Participating in Your Faith

Please be advised that the pastors are not the only ones responsible for your spiritual growth, but you, are responsible for your own spiritual growth. Hebrews 10:25 affirms: *"Not forsaking the assembling of ourselves together, as the manner of some is; but exhorting one another: and so much the more, as ye see the day approaching."*

Joining a Good Church

Here are a few pointers to keep in mind when making a decision to join a good church. Let's face it, everything that says church on it is not necessarily a church of the Lord Jesus Christ, for there are many false churches and teachers in the world. Below are some marks of a good church from Daniel Whyte's tract titled, *What to Do After You Enter Through the Door.*

A. The pastor preaches from the Word of God - the Bible—and he strives to practice what he preaches.
B. The church stands on the basics of the Christian faith. The basics of the Christian faith are:

- The Bible is inspired by God
- The Deity of Jesus Christ
- The Blood Atonement for sin by Jesus Christ
- Salvation by Faith in Jesus Christ
- The imminent Return of Jesus Christ

C. An emphasis is put on reaching out to others with the gospel of Jesus Christ.
D. The love of Jesus Christ is shown.

These are just a few marks of a good church. Pray and follow the Lord's leading.

CHAPTER 2
On Following the Crowd and Worldly Vanities

When I was younger I participated in this action of following the crowd to the extent of gaining attention by being the class clown. I was blessed with a good sense of humor, at least this was what I thought. I often used it to gain respect from my peers, even if it meant being disrespectful in most cases. Eventually, after many spankings, I learned to think for myself.

One day in particular, my father said something that really stuck with me (of course the discussion was before he gave me a lashing). You may be familiar with those words of encouragement your parents speak before you feel the sting of the strap. These ensemble of words are oftentimes more painful than the whipping itself. With a bold stern voice, my father exclaimed, *"Other people's kids might not get in trouble but you will. Learn to think for yourself. Use the good sense God gave you, girl. Lord knows it takes more than just good grades to make it in life."* And his last sentence, even though it seemed as a paragraph to me was: *"Those aren't your friends because a friend wouldn't encourage you to do something that would cause you to get in trouble. Always remember they are laughing at you not with you."*

This stayed with me throughout my school years. Frequently, I wondered how something so small could pack so much power. In any case, it caused me to straighten up and fly right. Now, I find myself expressing this same statement to others when they find themselves in trouble.

Just as Rev. Whyte so clearly articulated— do not follow the crowd; it is this crowd that was responsible for crucifying Jesus and it will do the same to you. God gave you a brain so that you may think for yourself—use it. Please take into account that a good leader must know how to follow before she can lead. In spite of this do not be deceived; there are always those who are willing to lead you to the bridge to jump off, but they will not follow after you. Yes, there are some instances in life which will require you to be a follower or vice versa. You must use your better judgment.

Worldly Vanity

According to the book of Ecclesiastes, King Solomon, the wisest man on the earth, came to the realization rather early that everything in life was all vanity. It takes most of us our whole lifetime to discover this reality.

Growing up in the church, the older saints had this to say: *"One life to live and it will soon be past, only what you do for Christ will last."* These words were constantly spoken to us. This powerful statement still resonates in my spirit today. I even believe that that statement is responsible for my avoiding many pitfalls.

Another axiom conveyed to me was *seeking the kingdom.* Matthew 6:33 declares: ***"But seek ye first the kingdom of God,*** *and his righteousness; and all these things shall be added unto you.* "Because this Scripture carries a great deal of weight the Saints regularly discussed it. We also explored another scripture, Proverbs 10:22. This scripture piggybacked Matthew 6:33 and it asserts: *"The blessing of the LORD, it maketh rich, and he addeth no sorrow with it."* This expresses the feeling one would have after being blessed by the Lord for his/her faithfulness. Why follow worldly vanities when we can have the Lord's blessings without sorrow?

CHAPTER 3
On Not Taking Education Seriously

I have been blessed with the opportunity of going back to school, which normally does not come back around a second time—I was awarded a scholarship for academics. An organization which was quite active in my community chose me as a recipient. Once I graduated from high school, I applied at a local junior college in my home-town. I got as far as enrolling, then the door closed due to no fault of my own. One of the board members in the organization who was responsible for disbursing funds withheld them from the school I was going to attend. I had no other means of paying for college and because of my ignorance with the financial aid process, I never started school. Eventually, I moved to Dallas for a fresh start. God blessed me with a great job at Boeing. Shortly after moving I received a phone call from the organization questioning me regarding the scholarship. The Board was under the impression that I had already received this award. It was just as I suspected, my scholarship had been stolen from me.

I was angry, but I eventually forgave, even though it took some time. I allowed this unfair act to detour me from going to school. Before long, I began to feel that I did not need an education, being that I was very young and making over twenty-five thousand dollars a year. How wrong I was. In time, all good things eventually come to an end. I labored for my employer four and a half years before getting laid-off because of the terrorist attack on September 11th. I had no idea what was in store for me.

I sought the Lord about this matter and He blessed me exceedingly. Normally, the unemployed would only receive benefits for six-months, but George Bush increased it to one year. Still uncertain, I continued to trust in God. I received a letter from Texas Workforce Commission. It stated that my employer had placed funding into a Trade Re-adjustment Assistance account and that I was an eligible candidate. This program was in efforts to help the unemployed gain skills or a trade in order to become employable again. In any case, it was no fault of ours that cutbacks had to be made. I was offered a free education to a two-year college, a four-year university or a vocational school.

Tarrant County College was my choice. I received TRA benefits for two years while attending there. I worked hard and succeeded in my studies. Going to school full-time was a requirement. I completed my Associate Arts in exactly two years, all the while maintaining honors. I transferred to another university after my tenure with TCC. Here, I was also blessed to have my education funded just as long as I maintained a good academic standing. I exceeded that which was required. Recently, I completed my Bachelor's and at this present time I am working on my Master's. Additionally, I believe that due to my faithfulness to God and my employer (also in my efforts of forgiving the person that stole my scholarship), I was blessed beyond measure. At this point in time, I continue to find favor with God in the area of my education.

So, you see my friend, the Scripture advises us to simply seek understanding in everything that we do. Proverbs 4:7 says: *"Wisdom is the principal thing; therefore get wisdom: and with all thy getting get understanding."*

What better way to apply such wisdom than in seeking your education? It will be counted as time well spent. To put it briefly, in order to get anywhere in life one must be educated and have proof that they are by possessing a diploma. Let me encourage you to take your education seriously, especially in this day and time. There is no guarantee that this opportunity will come around a second time. So, take advantage of it the first time around.

CHAPTER 4
On Having Sex, Of Any Kind,
Before Marriage

Sacred

Nowadays, too many young black women are finding themselves contemplating or participating in the act of pre-marital sex. Think twice before permitting your emotions to arouse your actions. In spite of your unconsciousness, this will result in your avoiding a mistake of a lifetime.

To be honest, for many men taking a woman's virginity and leaving her heartbroken is just a game of cat and mouse. Some women have learned this the hard way. Do not allow yourself to be placed in this situation because you will become bitter and remorseful. Your virginity is sacred; it's also something that you can never get back. Guard it as if your life depended on it. Below I would like to share with you my first encounter. Although personal, I feel compelled to share this with you in hopes that this will help you do the smart and wise thing, and to keep your virginity.

My First Encounter

My mother had me out of wedlock and at an early age. I was determined to break this generational curse. Being that I was the oldest of six children, this is one of many curses that skipped me. God and I made a pact that I would wait until I got married, something that I prayed about to Him quite often.

I got involved with a young man who I felt was Mr. Right. Of course, he turned out not to be that at all. Our relationship was great, at least until he got that itch—you know...sex. (This is the part in a relationship in which a man will show you his true colors.) He tried to persuade me to take it to the next level. In fact, one night at dinner amongst our friends and one of my relatives, I became the subject of our conversation. He relayed to my cousin that I was afraid. I explained, "It wasn't that I was afraid. I knew what I had been taught and I did not want to mess up my life. I knew the risks involved." Well, she tried to persuade me to go ahead and give in. I didn't feel comfortable about this at all, so I stood my ground. He called himself teaching me a lesson, I suppose, because after dinner he had my best friend's boyfriend to take him home. I went over to his house to talk shortly afterwards. Although I did not express it to anyone, I had a slight change of heart. Still not comfortable with the idea of giving myself to him, I began praying. Upon arriving at his house, I saw another female present.

The situation was very awkward and I was quite suspicious. Despite the fact that he was in his boxers, he conveyed to me that nothing happened and that he was about to go to bed when she stopped by. Besides, she was pregnant and was supposedly looking for her boyfriend, who was a friend of his. I had mixed emotions—excited that God saved me from making a horrible mistake in the following two ways: (1) this young lady being over to his house; and (2) my menstrual cycle began, which was very off schedule. I saw both as being signs of God's intervention. Although heart-broken, there was still this small amount of joy I had on the inside.

This young man and I parted ways. Our paths crossed one year later. He apologized for hurting me, but still insisted nothing happened. I forgave him. He also commended me on being such a strong woman, taking a stand for what I knew to be right. He suggested that we should try being more than friends, but I declined. Even though we lost touch we remain friends today.

There is nothing like your self-respect. Ladies, when you respect yourself you must demand others to do the same. Never let anyone encourage you to do something that you're not comfortable doing. If your significant other truly cares for you, then he will respect your wishes. And if he chooses not to wait, then you know that he is not the man that God has for you.

In addition, strengthen your relationship with God. If you do not already have a relationship with God, then consider doing so, because even when you are not thinking rationally, He's always sane.

CHAPTER 5
On Not Appreciating Your Parents and Family

Although I was raised by kinfolk (my Great Aunt and her family) and not my biological parents, I still enjoyed the benefits of such an environment. God placed me with the people He knew would give me the fundamentals of life, so I do not feel cheated in any way. As a matter of fact, I consider myself blessed. In many ways being nurtured by older people made me the person I am today.

We live in a day and time in which there are many negative influences, and as young ladies we have a tendency to follow our peers instead of the instructions of our parents. When I was younger I had the urge to do what others did, but thankfully I had parents who were concerned about me and who loved me enough to say NO. Some of you remember hearing these exact words: *"Just as long as you live under my roof you're going to do as I tell you."* Then, I felt restricted—I could not become an adult soon enough.

Quite soon, I saw the path that my peers had taken come to a dead end. Something became very clear to me—these were people (my peers) who tried to give me instruction and considered themselves wise and all the while their advice led to destruction. Thank God for parents who were in-tune and who saw to my avoiding those same mistakes that they made and the ones my peers were making.

Let me leave you with a word of advice: Do not have the attitude that you know it all. You must listen to others who have experienced life; they are just trying to impart wisdom into you. You never know, that very word that you may not want to listen to, just might help you make a critical decision. A wise person once advised me to take a word which was spoken to me and place it in a jar and set it on a shelf. Even if I didn't feel that it was important, tuck it away. They assured me that I would put it to good use sooner or later.

For the most part, I find it encouraging speaking to those much older because they give me great advice. Just as Rev. Whyte expressed if you do not already, consider spending time with your parents or grandparents to discuss life. You just might learn that you all share something in common.

CHAPTER 6
On Leaving Home Too Soon

Safer In the Nest

There are times when we, as females, feel that we are ready to leave the nest. But after analyzing the world around us, we soon find that it's just a fancy. Others who have acted upon such a decision almost immediately learn that they, too, should have waited, due to circumstances that arised which they did not plan for. This brings me to the following point: Do not allow anyone to encourage you to leave home if you are not ready, and if you do not have to. The world can be very cold and if you are not prepared, you will end up being overtaken.

The safest place other than being in the will of God is staying in the nest. After all, the idea of being out on your own is not to return, if possible. If your living environment is not conducive then I would advise you to seek shelter elsewhere, but only if you are endangered, and not because you choose not to comply with your parents' rules.

My intent is not to discourage you from moving out, but to prompt you to think long and hard about your options. With all things considered, one of the joys of embracing such an exciting event in your life is being ready. As mentioned earlier, one of the marks of a mature woman is making sure you are able to handle things on your own without falling apart.

Rev. Whyte mentioned six marks of a mature woman. I encourage you to read them and to take heed to them.

CHAPTER 7
On Not Having Clear Direction in Life

Rev. Whyte pointed out one way to guarantee that your time is not wasted is by mapping out goals and following each step precisely. Each accomplishment you achieve will bring about a great reward. This gets you one step closer to accomplishing your next goal, and before you know it the idea of living life to its fullest has arrived, without regrets.

So, young ladies, use wisdom concerning life and all that it has to offer. But more importantly include and consult God. He's concerned about you in every area of your life. Just in case you are not convinced, take the following Scriptures and hide them away in your heart: Third John 2 says: *"Beloved, I wish above all things that thou mayest prosper and be in health, even as thy soul prospereth."* Also, 2 Peter 1:3 reassures: *"According as his divine power hath given unto us all things that pertain unto life and godliness..."*

As I draw to a close, it's with a cheerful heart that I express this: pray and seek the Lord daily. As you embark upon this journey of new found discoveries, I promise that you will never find yourself bored. Just keep your hand in God's hand, your mind stayed upon Him, and your heart in tune with His.

"It's a tragedy of our time that many become parents before they cease being children."

A Word to Parents

Dear Parents:

I trust that you are doing well today.

King Solomon, the wisest man who ever lived, tells us in Proverbs 22:6: *"Train up a child in the way he should go and when he is old he will not depart from it."* That is a promise from God, that if we, without letting up, teach, train, and discipline our children while they are young, if we show them the right way according to the Scriptures, then they will not depart from this training. This is not to say they will not make mistakes, but you have God's Word that they will always remember the training they received from you.

Our daughters are special and they are much tougher than we oftentimes give them credit for. As a father of six girls, I must admit I am not as hard on my girls as I am on my boys. But as a father, I also know that it is my job to prepare them to face the world on their own, and to be able to make wise decisions.

We want our daughters to be knowledgeable about the world that they live in, so they can go out without fear or feeling they have to compromise their standards to survive. And, of course, we do not want them to make the same mistakes that we did in our younger years.

However, sad to say, I have noticed that many parents are afraid to look their children in their eyes and share with them the facts of life. Many parents are afraid to take and exercise their God-given authority over their children. I am not going to go into all the reasons why. If, however, one of the reasons is because you do not know where to begin, may I lovingly encourage you to begin with the Bible and this little book.

Have a time of prayer and Bible reading with your children in the morning and at night. Then, may I encourage you to take this book and read it with your daughters—discuss its contents with them and help them to apply the life principles contained therein. Read it with them more than once. Internalize the eternal principles in the book yourself, while helping them to internalize it as well. See this book as a signpost for their lives as it will help you to show them things to avoid so they will not mess up their lives.

Pass it on to your grand-daughters and to any other young black woman in your life, for the truths contained therein are invaluable.

Blessings,

Daniel Whyte III

"Some are so anxious to give their children what they didn't have that they have neglected to give them what they had."

RESOURCES

BOOKS

1. *The Power of Being a Woman: Embracing the Triumph of the Feminine Spirit*, by Michelle McKinney Hammond

2. *Understanding the Purpose and Power of Women*, by Myles Munroe

3. *True Woman: The Beauty and Strength of a Godly Woman*, by Susan Hunt

4. *The Quest for Character*, by John MacArthur

5. *A Jewel in His Crown - Rediscovering Your Value as a Woman of Excellence*, by Priscilla Shirer

6. *Beautiful in God's Eyes: The Treasures of the Proverbs 31 Woman*, by Elizabeth George

7. *Letters to Young Black Women*, by Daniel Whyte III with Meriqua & Daniella Whyte

8. *The Girl God Wants*, by Daniella Whyte

RESOURCES

WEBSITES

1. www.LProof.org — Living Proof Ministries with Beth Moore

2. www.PurposeDrivenLife.com — Purpose Driven Life with Rick Warren

3. www.MichelleHammond.com — Michelle McKinney Hammond

4. www.JoyceMeyer.org — Joyce Meyer

5. www.GoingBeyond.com — Priscilla Shirer

6. www.SisterLessons.com — Bestselling Author, Speaker, Coach, and CEO, Natasha Munson

7. www.LetterstoYoungBlackWomen.org — Site for the Amazon.com bestselling book, *Letters to Young Black Women*

7 Great Thoughts for Young Black Women

"If you are not as close to God as you used to be, who moved?"
~Author Unknown

"The perfect church service would be one we were almost unaware of. Our attention would have been on God."
~C.S. Lewis

"The real ornament of a woman is her character and her purity."
~Mohandas Gandhi

"There come times when I have nothing more to tell God. If I were to continue to pray in words, I would have to repeat what I have already said. At such times it is wonderful to say to God, 'May I be in Thy presence, Lord? I have nothing more to say to Thee, but I do love to be in Thy presence.'"
~O. Hallesby

"If you don't like something change it; if you can't change it, change the way you think about it."
~Mary Engelbreit

"People grow through experience if they meet life honestly and courageously. This is how character is built."
~Eleanor Roosevelt

"Life is not the way it's supposed to be. It's the way it is. The way you deal with it is what makes the difference."
~Virginia Satir

VISIT US ON THE WEB AT:
www.7ThingsYoungBlackWomenDoToMessUpTheirLives.com

9609443R0

Made in the USA
Lexington, KY
13 May 2011